THE ANCIENT BLACK HEBREWS VOL II

THE FORENSIC PROOF SIMPLY EXPLAINED

POMEGRANATE PUBLISHING

LONDON

THE ANCIENT BLACK HEBREWS
VOL II

THE FORENSIC PROOF SIMPLY EXPLAINED

GERT MULLER

POMEGRANATE PUBLISHING
LONDON

**POMEGRANATE PUBLISHING
LONDON**

TABLE OF CONTENTS

INTRODUCTION: PURPOSE OF THIS VOLUME

The point of this volume is to explain, in simple language, the basis of ancestry determination used by forensic anthropologists, with a view to applying this to the ancient skeletal remains from Israel. We shall see whether or not they agree with the conclusions of Volume 1 which was based on Biblical data. It concluded that the Old Testament Hebrews were Black. We shall do this by reviewing reports on these human remains written by forensic anthropologists. These remains are mainly from the Iron Age ancient city of **Lachish** in southern Israel (the ancient kingdom of Judah) and the Hellenistic and Roman period desert site of **En Gedi** (Judah was called Judea in this period). Before we proceed to the forensic chapters we shall recap the conclusions of Vol 1. We shall then establish what it is we should be looking for to confirm or deny the conclusions of volume 1.

CHAPTER 1: THE SHEMITES

The Ancestors of Shem

The story of the Hebrews in Genesis ultimately begins with the creation of Adam and his being moved to the Garden of Eden. Adam was not a Hebrew but human social groups tend to compound the creation of humanity with the ethnogenesis of their own group. In verses 8 and 10-14 we read a description of the location of Eden:

> And the LORD God planted a garden eastward in Eden; and there he put the man he had formed...
> And a river went out of Eden to water the garden; and from thence it was parted, and became into four heads.
> The name of the first is **Pison: that is it which compasseth the whole land of Havilah**, where there is gold;
> And the gold of that land is good: there is bdellium and onyx stone.
> **And the name of the second river is Gihon: the same is it that compasseth the whole land of Ethiopia**. And the name of the third river is Hiddekel: that is it which **goeth towards the east of Assyria. And the fourth is Euphrates**

The book *Eden: the Biblical Garden Discovered in East Africa* (by Gert Muller, Pomegranate Publishing 2013) explains that this four river system is a reference to certain of the Nile tributaries in Central-Eastern Sudan and Ethiopia. **Havilah**, in the Table of Nations (Gen. 10), is a son of Cush, the Hebrew equivalent of 'Ethiopia'. This implies that Havilah was in the region of Cush or Ethiopia. Evidence is also presented, from the Table of Nations, to show another **Asshur** (translated in Gen. 2 KJV as 'Assyria') in the part of Arabia opposite Ethiopia. Many of the Biblical names in that part of Arabia, provided in the Table of Nations, also occur on the other side of the Red Sea in Ethiopia. **It makes it quite possible the Hebrews thought there was an Asshur in Ethiopia as well.** The Euphrates in ancient times was said to have its source in Ethiopia. The names Hiddekel (Tigris) and Parat (Euphrates) in Hebrew are indicative of descriptive qualities of 'rapid' and 'fruitful' respectively. These descriptions happen to match the Tekkeze and Gash rivers of Ethiopia which form a fertile plain like Mesopotamia. Even medieval rabbis thought that Eden was located in Ethiopia as we are about to see.

According to Genesis humanity only spread out over the earth after the Flood. Before this the nine generations after Adam lived in Eden, the area the garden was located. After the first couple were expelled from the garden they lived in this area. The *Book of Jasher* was written by a Jewish rabbi in the medieval period and purports to be the ancient '*Book of Jasher*' referred to in the Old Testament. It claims that in the days **before** Noah God sent a flood to the antediluvian people to warn them of their wicked ways:

> Jash 2:6 And the Lord caused the **waters of the river Gihon to overwhelm them,** and he destroyed and

consumed them, and **he destroyed the third part of the earth,** and notwithstanding this, the sons of men did not turn from their evil ways, and their hands were yet extended to do evil in the sight of the Lord.
http://www.johnpratt.com/items/docs/jasher.html#Jash_6

The Gihon, as stated in Genesis, was the river that **'compasseth the whole land of Ethiopia'**. The word 'earth' in Hebrew is *erets*. It can mean 'the whole earth', 'ground', 'region' or 'inhabitants'. The only way a third of the 'inhabitants' of the 'earth' could have been killed by Gihon flooding is if all of humanity was imagined to have lived by that river. If they meant a third of the 'region' of Eden then it must have been located in the neighbourhood of Cush. Either way it makes ALL Biblical figures from Adam to Noah East Africans.

The Shemites

Noah's children Ham, Shem and Japheth were East Africans. The descendants of Shem moved to West Asia while the descendants of Japheth moved to the vast region of Eurasia. In Eurasia the Black Japhethites turned White. This probably happened by giving birth to White babies, with straight hair, as in the picture below. **These babies were not albinos.** Although it is rare this still happens amongst Sub-Saharan Africans to this day.

Figure 1 Nigerian family with White baby
who has straight, blonde hair

The Shemites became the aboriginal West Asians like the **Elamites** and **Black Syrians.** Nimrod, the son of Cush, followed the Shemites to West Asia and set up camp in southern Mesopotamia (see the *Black Sumer* trilogy). Later the Japhethites moved from Eurasia to this region. This led to a gradual whitening of the West Asians during antiquity (see *Unmistakably Black: Sculptures and Paintings from the World's First Civilizations* by Anu M'Bantu, Pomegranate Publishing 2013).

Figure 2 A Black Elamite Persian and a White Japhetic Persian

From Shem also came **Eber**, the father of **Joctan**. The latter was the father of the aboriginal people of Arabia who can still be found in parts of central, southern and eastern Arabia speaking South Semitic languages like Mahri and Shahari. They are of obvious Black descent today (as seems evident from their pictures) with hair resembling that of First Australians. This strongly suggests Joctan, Eber and Shem were supposed to be Black in the mind of the original authors of Genesis.

Abraham's Descendants

Abraham was descended from Shem and Eber which strongly suggests that he too was Black, according to the story. His grandson Jacob used stones for pillows suggesting that his hair was thick and Afro enough to form a comfortable cushion between his scalp and the rocks. Jacob's son, Joseph, was mistaken for an Egyptian (African), by the rest of Jacob's family after being sold into slavery in his youth. Jacob's distant descendant was Moses who was also mistaken for an Egyptian in Midian. Moses had his hand turned white as part of an impressive miracle. Turning

Figure 3 A Mahra man with complexion
contrasting white costume

type 6 skin into type 1 skin would be the most impressive
miracle. This strongly suggests Moses had a complexion like
Naomi Campbell's (see *The Ancient Black Hebrews Vol I*). The
logic of the Hebrew Levitical laws excludes types 1-4 from
the general complexion range.

Figure 4 A man of the Beni Himyar,
descended from the ancient
Himyarites, related to the Mahra

Figure 5 Israel, next to Egypt, in
relation to Africa and Europe

The Nazarites were described as 'red' like 'earth', clearly a dark red, which came to approximate a 'coal black' as a result of famine. This is clearly a case of starvation-induced hyper-pigmentation. Skin types 5 and 6 are more susceptible to this condition and only type 6 could produce a complexion that approximates 'coal'. Other Old Testament figures like Job also complained of disease-induced hyper-pigmentation. David and Solomon were described as the same 'red' like 'earth' as the Nazarites.

All of this tells us that the ancient Hebrews **of the Old Testament** were a Black people like other aboriginal peoples of West Asia. It gives credibility to the many paintings of Black Christ and Madonna that can be found in the oldest churches of Europe and Asia Minor. It also places in context some of the images found in early medieval synagogues in West Asia and Europe. When we consider the geographical context of Israel, in relation to Africa and Europe, there is nothing surprising about this.

CHAPTER 2: HOW CAN WE TELL?

How Do We Know What A Skull Would Have Looked Like?

How do we know what a skull would have looked like in real life? The average human can tell the difference between the skulls of a lion, a gorilla and a human. They can do this by looking at the shape of the skulls and comparing them to their living counterparts. They can see which one has the massive predatory teeth, shape of nose and general skull shape that would be expected of a lion. They can also see which two skulls have a greater similarity with the expectation that these are the gorilla and human. The gorilla skull would be much bigger, with a backward slanting face and bigger, sharper canines. The reader will have little difficulty distinguishing them below.

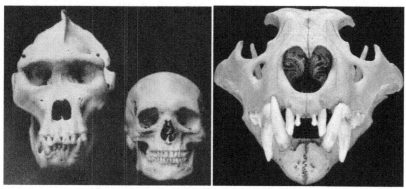

Figure 6 Skull of gorilla, human and lion.
It is easy to pick which is which

At a more refined level a forensic anthropologist can tell whether the owner of a human skull, when alive, looked more like Sub-Saharan Africans, Europeans or East Asians. If the skull has a blend of traits they can detect this too.

The differences in appearance between people indigenous to Europe, East Asia and Sub-Saharan Africa are due to climatic adaptation. North Africa, West, South and South-East Asia are zones where people of different continental appearance have been mixing for at least three thousand years. Other works by Pomegranate Publishing such as the *Black Sumer* trilogy, *Racial Unity of the Ancient Egyptians and Nubians,* and *Black Gods and Civilization of Ancient India* show that the people of the mixing zones approximated Sub-Saharan African appearance before 3000 years ago.

The Role of Climate

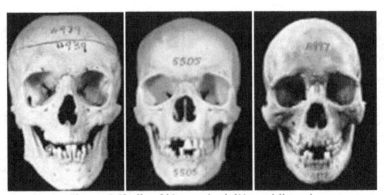

Figure 7 Skulls of 'Caucasian', 'Negroid', and East Asiatic, in that order

Climate influences the shape of the skull and face. We know this because of the many studies that have shown that the shape of these places consistently vary with climate. Because of this we can examine an ancient skeleton and tell whether it is indigenous to a particular kind of climate.

There is a considerable amount of variety within a population. This is why it is ideal to have at least 30 skulls of one sex from a population to see the dominant trend. **It is about trends and not absolutes. There are no absolute human populations. In zoology a race is a sub-group, within a species, whose defining characteristics are absolute. This is what is meant by 'there's no such thing as race', a claim that, if misunderstood, has the potential to cause more confusion than it clears up. It is not intended to prevent us from learning about the physical appearance of skeletal individuals and populations.** The variety within populations is something we shall see repeatedly as we go through the different skull features and how climate influences their shape.

There are three zoological rules which are responsible for much of the geographic variety in physical appearance amongst humans. **Allen's Rule states that as one moves from warmer to colder climates they will find the length of limbs decreasing in native races within a warm-blooded species.** This predicts longer limbs in tropical and sub-tropical animals in comparison to their temperate counterparts of the same species. **Bergmann's Rule states that as one moves from warmer to colder climates they will find the total body size of native races within a warm-**

blooded species increasing. This predicts smaller animals in tropical and sub-tropical climates, in comparison to their temperate counterparts of the same species. **Gloger's Rule states that as one moves from colder to warmer climates they will find an increase in outer covering melanin in native races within a warm-blooded species**. This predicts dark-coloured outer coverings in tropical and sub-tropical animals in comparison to their temperate counterparts of the same species.

What is a Native Group?

Rules have exceptions but even they can often be explained by knowledge of other rules or by knowledge of the exceptional population's history. **Just because people are located in warm climates it does not make them warm-adapted**. One has to know how long they have been resident in the tropical or sub-tropical geographic zone. White South Africans, for instance, are of European origin and began arriving in the sub-tropics just over three centuries ago. There has not been enough time for adaptations according to Allen, Bergmann and Gloger's Rules. The indigenous people of tropical Central America originally came from the Bering Straits, far to the north. They have made a few adaptations because they have been there for many thousands of years but their physique still shows **clear signs of cold-adapted origins**. The peoples of tropical South-East Asia and Polynesia are, in their physique, also cold-adapted. The original peoples of this region were Negritos and Melanesians who have **warm-adapted physiques and have**

heavily pigmented skin. This is in keeping with Allen, Bergmann and Gloger. Many Indo-European-speaking ethnic groups in and near sub-tropical West Asia, such as Persians and Afghans, have ancestors who came from further north over 3000 years ago. Logically the Semitic-speaking groups in West Asia were also affected by their presence because of inter-marriage. There was also settlement of Indo-European- and Hurrian-speakers in Syro-Palestine (see e-book *The Black God and Goddess of the Bible* by Gert Muller, Pomegranate Publishing 2013) We need to bear in mind the presence of cold-originating populations in hot climates when we look at the evidence correlating climate with the skeletal structure of present-day populations.

What Forensic Anthropologists Say About Climate and Human Physique

> Several morphological features, such as stature, nose form, body build, head form, etc., are affected by variable climatic stresses (Weidenreich, 1945; Hulse, 1971).

"Climate and Head Form in India" by S Bharati, S Som, P Bharati, TS Vasulu, in, *American Journal of Human Biology 13* 2001 p626

> The strongest findings have linked climate to body weight, body proportions, **skin pigmentation**, and **relative nose and head width**.

"Human Nasal Protrusion, Latitude and Climate" by JM Carey and MT Steegman, in, *AJPA 56* 1981 p317

On the cold-adapted proportions of Native Central Americans see p423-447

"Body Proportions in Late Pleistocene Europe and Modern Human Origins" by Trenton W Holliday, in *Journal of Human Evolution 32* 1997

http://www.merriam-webster.com/dictionary/allen%27s%20rule

http://www.merriam-webster.com/dictionary/bergmann%27s%20rule

http://www.merriam-webster.com/dictionary/gloger%27s%20rule

CHAPTER 3: WHAT SKULL SHAPE TELLS US

Cephalic Index

What is it about skull shape that informs us about the climate to which the possessor was indigenous? We need to understand that the purpose of the skull is to protect the brain. One of the crucial ways in which it does this is by regulating its temperature. In hot places the primary objective is to allow the skull to lose heat. In cold places it is to retain heat. **People indigenous to hot places tend to have smaller, more elongated skulls because oblong shapes lose heat better than round ones. People indigenous to cold places tend to have larger, rounder skulls because these retain heat better.** These expectations are based on the rules of Allen and Bergmann.

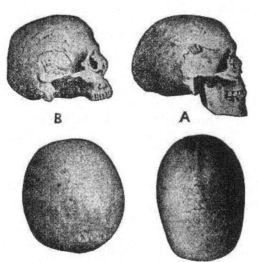

Figure 8 Dolichocephalic and brachycephalic skulls

Cephalic index = (max breadth of skull/max length) x 100

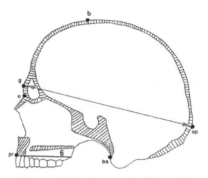

Figure 9 Maximum skull length

Narrower skulls, in relation to their length are called **dolichocephalic**. Wider ones are called **brachycephalic** and those that are intermediate are called **mesocephalic**. According to Bergmann's rule the first tend to be found in warmer climates and the second in colder climates. Not everyone in a warm population is dolichocephalic. **Within a population there is considerable variety of cephalic index.** An example is amongst the Howells database sample of the first 30 male Norwegian skulls the range is from 70.3 (very dolichocephalic) to 82.1 (quite brachycephalic). **This is greater than the difference between the average Norwegian male index (74.8) and average Zulu or Dogon male index (72.7 and 77.2).** Like we said earlier; **it is about dominating trends not absolute types. This is what is meant by 'there is no such thing as race'. It is not intended to prevent us from learning about the physical appearance of skeletal individuals and populations.**

The average index for the population, however, tends to follow climatic patterns although there is some overlap. Part of the overlap is explained by the role humidity plays in influencing the shape of the skull. Lower humidity has the same effect as high temperatures hence the most dolichocephalic skulls are found in places of **dry heat** while the most brachycephalic skulls are found in places of **wet cold**. If a dolichocephalic group is found in Europe it would probably be located in a **dry cold** zone and would display a moderate form. If a brachycephalic group is to be found in Africa it would probably be in a **wet heat** zone and would display a moderate form.

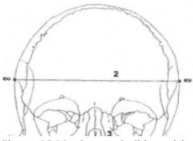

Figure 10 Maximum skull breadth

A study published in 2009 used 33 measurements from skull samples of populations native to every climatic and geographic zone to see which ones had **stronger correlations with temperature and humidity**. They produced a table showing that the strongest correlations were with **biauricular breadth**, **maximum cranial breadth** and **bizygomatic breadth**, in that order ("Climate Signatures in the Morphological Differentiation of Worldwide Modern Human Populations" by Mark Hubbe,

Tsuneko Hanihara and Katerina Harvati, in, *The Anatomical Record* 292 (2009) table 4 p1724).

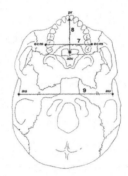

Figure 11 View from under the skull. The central measurement is biauricular breadth

Let us look at the cephalic index, maximum skull breadth and biauricular breadth of skulls from ancient Judah and compare them to populations from around the world. In the process we shall see which measurements are better at distinguishing warm-adapted and cold-adapted skull samples.

Skulls from Judea

The skulls from Judah, southern Israel, come from the settlements of Lachish, and En Gedi. Lachish was an important city in ancient Israel and its skulls are thought to date back to the Iron Age around 700 BC (measurements of Lachish skulls are taken from data in "Analysis of Crania from Tell Duweir Using Multiple Discriminant Functions" by SOY Keita, *American Journal of Physical Anthropology (AJPA) 75* (1988) p375-390).

Figure 12 Map of Israel showing En Gedi
near the Dead Sea and Lake Tiberius
to the north

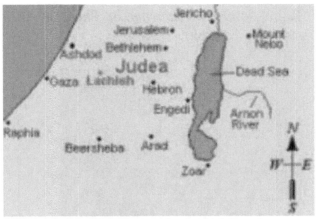

Figure 13 Map showing Lachish in red

Other skulls were from Safed, a small town in Galilee, northern Israel. The measurements are from *Tell el Hesy (Lachish)* by William Matthew Flinders Petrie, Cambridge University Press 2013 (reprint of early 20th century work) p34. Skulls from the desert village of En Gedi date back to Hellenistic and Roman periods (300-66 BC; 50 BC-100 AD). The measurements of male crania from Hellenistic and Roman En Gedi are from a team of Israeli forensic anthropologists who published the paper: "Skeletal Remains of Jews from the Hellenistic, Roman and Byzantine Periods in Israel I – Metric Analysis" by B Arensburg, MS Goldstein, H Nathan and Y Rak, in, *Bulletins et Mémoires de la Société d'anthropologie de Paris 7* xxxi 1980a p178-80. All measurements, unless specified, are the first 30 males from the Howells world-wide database populations. It can be downloaded at: http://web.utk.edu/~auerbach/HOWL.htm. It is in Microsoft Excel format and our figures can be cross-checked in a matter of seconds.

27

Cephalic Index

Table 1

Population males (30 skulls) unless stated	Cephalic Index
Teita, Kenyan	70.5
Zulu, South African	72.7
Dogon, Malian	77.2
Norse, Norwegian	74.8
Zalavar, Hungarian	76.2
Berg, Austrian	82.4
Gizeh, 26-30th dynasty Egyptian	74.7
Lachish, 700 BC Judah (61)	74.5
Hellenistic Period Judean (35)	78.1
Roman Period Judean (25)	79.1

Above is a table of cephalic indices of Sub-Saharan African and European male population samples of 30 skulls from the Howells database. Table 1 illustrates that while cephalic index does **indicate** which populations are warm-adapted and which are cold-adapted it does not **determine. An example is that the Norwegians have a lower (more warm-adapted) cephalic index than the Dogon.** We nonetheless note that the Lachish skulls are within the Sub-Saharan range. It indicates that they are warm-adapted.

Maximum Skull Breadth

When we only use maximum skull breadth the overlap vanishes and we have a more efficient distinguisher as seen in Table 2. **Like all measurements skull breadth shows plenty of variety within a population sample.** In fact the range in the **first 30 individual Norwegian male skulls (131-145)** of the Howells database is greater than the difference between the average Norwegian measurement (**140.3**) and the average Zulu measurement (**135.3**). **Sub-Saharan Africans usually show greater range in measurements (first 30 Zulu males, 125-145):**

Table 2

Populations (30 skulls)	Max Skull Breadth
Norse, Norwegian	140.3
Zalavar, Hungarian	141.1
Berg, Austrian	149
Poundbury, Roman Britain (50)	146
Teita, Kenyan	129.8
Zulu, South African	135.3
Gabon, West Africa (41)	135.6
Dogon, Malian	137.3
C-Group Nubian (28)	135.3
1st dynasty Abydos Egyptian (54)	136.2
Gizeh, 26-30th dynasty Egyptian	138.7
Lachish, 700 BC Judah (61)	138.5
En Gedi Hellenistic Judean (35)	142.3
En Gedi Roman Judean (25)	144.8
Safed, Palestine(1500 BC) (7)	137

Safed, Palestine (Roman) (14)	133

The Safed measurements are from *Tell el Hesy (Lachish)* by William Matthew Flinders Petrie, Cambridge University Press 2013 (reprint of early 20th century work) p34
Nubian, Gabon, Abydos, Lachish and Poundbury measurements are from Keita (1988), full reference in future chapter.

This metric (measured) trait is good at separating Sub-Saharan African from European population samples in the Howells database. The Sub-Saharan upper limit, **from these samples**, is **137.3** while the European lower limit is **140.3**. The Norwegians are from a dry climate which makes the skull narrower than most cold-adapted populations (Hubbe et al 2009 p1732). Despite being from so far north they are a good lower limit for cold-adapted populations. There is a difference of exactly **3 points (mm)** between the European and African neighbouring limits. C-Group Nubians are indistinguishable from Sub-Saharan Africans **in this measurement**. 1st dynasty Abydos Egyptians are also within this range but Gizeh 26-30th dynasty Egyptians are somewhat outside the range by **1.4 points** and away from the European range by **1.6 points** (mm). We could conclude, **on this limited evidence**, conclude that **Late Lower Egyptians were 53.3% African and 46.6 % European (1.6/3 = African component, 1.4/3 = European component)**. It suggests cold-adapted intermixture took place between the 1st and 30th dynasty.

Using the same principle the Safed male skulls from the 18th dynasty Galilee (1500 BC) are within the Sub-Saharan

African range (129.8-137.3). The **Lachish Judah** male skulls **(138.5)** lie outside the range by **1.2 points** and away from the European range by **1.8 points**. We could conclude, **on this limited evidence**, that the people of **Lachish were 60% African and 40% European**. The skulls from **Hellenistic and Roman En Gedi, on this limited evidence**, would be **firmly within the European range**. It should be remembered that these estimates are based on the **assumption** that the Afro-type population concerned was like the Dogon and the Euro-type population was like the Norwegians, **in this measurement**.

These statistical amounts are intended to be guides only and not absolutes because they are only based on one trait. What we can say with more certainty is that **on the basis of this trait alone** the Lachish sample was more African than European. One measurement, however, is likely to create this kind of uncertainty which is why we shall proceed to use others.

Horizontal Circumference

Table 3

Populations males (30)	Horizontal circumference
Poundbury, Roman Britain (61)	537.1
Gabon, West Africa (41)	501.3
Badarian Pre-dynastic Egypt (22)	503.0
Teita (30)	508.7

Abydos, 1st dynasty (54)	511.28
Kerma Nubian (52)	513.7
Lachish, Judah (700 BC)	516.8

All measurements from Keita (1988) p383

We would expect a warm-adapted population to have a smaller head size than a cold-adapted population, **following Bergmann's Rule**. Horizontal circumference, or the distance around the head at the forehead, is a good measure of this. Because they are from further north the Kerma Nubians are probably closer to the Afro-type involved than the more southerly Teita or Gabon. We do not, however, have a Euro-type from further south than Britain. This will skew the proportions in favour of the African component (which would support the present author's theory but we must put **honesty** and **fairness** before skewed support). In order to produce a more accurate picture of proportion we shall use the Teita measurement because they are from further south than the Afro-population involved just as the Roman Britons are from further north than the Euro-type population involved.

There is a **28.4 point** difference between the horizontal circumference of the Teita **(508.7)** and that of the Roman Britons **(537.1)**. Lachish is **8.1 points** away from the Teita as compared to **28.4 points** away from Roman Britons. **This would make the Lachish people approximately 71.5% African and 28.5% European**. This is **assuming** the Euro-type population involved was more like the Roman Britons and the Afro-type population was like the Nubians.

32

Biauricular Breadth

Biauricular breadth was the **strongest indicator of climatic adaptation** in the 2009 study earlier cited (Hubbe et al 2009). In table 4a we show the average biauricular breadths of samples from around the world as compared to those from ancient Palestine.

Table 4a

Population males (30)	Biauricular Br
Norse, Norwegian	123.7
Zalavar, Hungarian	123.5
Berg, Austrian	129.2
Pounbury, Roman Britain (50)	126.3
Andaman Islander	110.3
Bushman, South African	113.7
Zulu, South African	116.3
Dogon, Malian	115.1
Gabon (41)	115.1
Teita, Kenyan	117.5
Kerma Nubian (89)	118.2
C-Group Nubian (20)	119.3
Abydos, 1st dynasty Egyptian (54)	119.6
Gizeh 26-30th dynasty Egypt	118.3
Safed (1500 BC) Palestine (7)	115
Safed, Roman Palestine (14)	116
Lachish, Judah (700 BC) (61)	119.2

The 18th dynasty Palestinians and the Lachish Judah samples are within the range created by Sub-Saharan African and Nubian measurements. **This strongly suggests that they were warm- and not cold-adapted.** This specific trait does not suggest inter-mixture with cold-adapted populations. It also does not indicate this for Late Dynastic Lower Egyptians who had been mixing with Asiatics for well over a thousand years. Perhaps this measurement only indicates whether one is more warm- or cold adapted but does not indicate mixture so well. Lachish does not differ at all from the Nubians for this measurement. Biauricular breadths were not available for Hellenistic and Roman period En Gedi. The Roman period sample from Safed indicates Judeans were a warm-adapted population, **in contradiction** to the maximum skull breadths of Roman period En Gedi.

Table 4b

First Australian	118.9
Indigenous Tasmanian	**124.6**
Tolai, New Britain (Melanesian)	120.2
Mokapu, Hawaii Polynesian	128.1
Easter Island, Polynesia	123.8
South Maori (18)	128.1
Guam, Micronesia	130.3
North Japan	124.6
Philippines	124
Arikara Nation, North Dakota	131
Peru, Native South Americans	124.8
Inuit	126.8

With the exception of Indigenous Tasmanians the Australo-Melanesians are differentiated from the Polynesians, South-East Asians and Native North and South Americans. **Biauricular breadth separates the warm-adapted from the cold-adapted, even if they currently inhabit tropical and sub-tropical locations like the Philippines and Guam.** The Tasmanians are the only Black exception to this separation in the entire Howells world-wide database. Black skin is an excellent indicator of warm-adaptation. The exception can be explained by the fact that Tasmania has a temperate climate and the original inhabitants probably arrived at the same time as the First Australians. This was at least 50 000 years ago. This is enough time to develop aspects of a cold-adapted skull shape. Tasmanians looked like First Australians with Afro hair. They became extinct in 1876 as a result of British colonial genocidal policies.

Figure 14 An Original Tasmanian

Conclusion

Maximum skull breadth, horizontal circumference and biauricular breadth are measurements which **separate Africans from Europeans** in the Howells world-wide database. They are identified as **strong indicators of warm- and cold-adaptation** by a world-wide study of 2009. All three indicate either a sub-tropically-adapted Afro-type population in Safed and Lachish or a mixed population with a major Afro-type component. **A reasonable inference, following Gloger's Rule, would be that the people of Judah had heavily pigmented skins that complimented their sub-tropical adaptation.**

Biauricular breadth is the most efficient separator of warm-adapted populations from cold-adapted ones. All living groups in the Howells database with biauricular breadths under 120 are either African or Australo-Melanesian. **Their heavily pigmented skin is an obvious indicator of their warm-adaptation.** Such a powerful separator groups the people of 18th dynasty Safed, 7th century BC Lachish, and Roman period Safed with the warm-adapted peoples of this world.

What Forensic Anthropologists Say about Skull Shape

In the 19th century, **two "ecogeographical rules"** were proposed, hypothesizing that **total body size within warm-blooded species would increase as temperatures fell (Bergmann, 1847), while the size**

of body extremities would decrease (Allen, 1877). These ecogeographical rules are each consistent with fundamental thermodynamic principles, and are based on the assumption that variation in the ratio of surface area (the site of heat loss) to body mass or volume (the site of heat production) allows adaptation to different thermal environments
"Ecogeographical Associations Between Climate and Human Body Composition: Analyses Based on Anthropometry and Skinfolds" by Jonathan CK Wells AJPA 147 2012 p169

Thus, **cephalic index** is apparently correlated with climatic stress and follows the ecological rules of Allen and Bergmann. It is generally expected that **under cold stress, the most advantageous head shape would be of a round type (brachycephalic), since this most closely approximates the spherical ideal. Under hot climatic conditions, a long head would be more advantageous.** In reality, **there are numerous exceptions to these expectations.**
Climate and Head Form in India by S Bharati, S Som, P Bharati, TS Vasulu, in, *American Journal of Human Biology 13* 2001 p626

Based on a sample of 339 populations, the magnitude of the index is statistically different between zones of predominantly **dry heat, wet heat, wet cold and dry cold.** It is argued that the occupation of cold climates is one of the **circumstances increasing the frequency of brachycephaly through time.**

"Head Form and Climatic Stress" by Kenneth Beals, in, *AJPA 37* 1972p85

Table 4 lists the Fst values calculated for the entire set of craniometric measurements and for each variable separately...**Only three neurocranial measurements showed high Fst values, and all reflect cranial breadth (XCB, XFB, and AUB)**.

"Climate Signatures in the Morphological Differentiation of Worldwide Modern Human Populations" by Mark Hubbe, Tsuneko Hanihara and Katerina Harvati, in, *The Anatomical Record 292* (2009) p1724

In the actual table bizygomatic breadth ZYB **(0.4368)** had a higher Fst than maximum frontal breadth XFB **(0.3182)**. XCB are the forensic symbols for maximum cranial breadth, XFB maximum frontal breadth and AUB biauricular breadth. Fst is a measure of population differentiation with a genetic basis.

CHAPTER 4: WHAT THE NOSE TELLS US

Nasal Index

What is it about the skeletal nose that informs us about the climate to which the possessor was indigenous? We need to understand the purpose of the human nose to answer this question. It is a chamber that captures air for our consumption from the external environment converting it to the right temperature and humidity for the body. In environments that are hot and moist the nose has to do the least amount of converting for suitability. As a result the nostrils are shaped so that air can enter with less contact and interference. This leads to round nostrils and, broad, low, short noses. The opposite extreme would be areas which are cold and dry. Here the nose has to do the most converting to make air the right temperature and humidity for the body. This leads to almond shaped nostrils and narrow, long, high noses.

$$\text{Nasal index} = (\text{breadth}/\text{height}) \times 100$$

Where there is a warm climate and low humidity the noses tend to be narrower. An example of this would be some prehistoric Rift Valley Kenyans who, before the arrival of Bantu-speakers from Central and West Africa, had noses that were so narrow the European examiners mistook them for a Euro-type (*Stone Age Races of Kenya* by Louis SB Leakey, Oxford University Press 1933). The forensic anthropologist Philip Rightmire, in a highly influential paper, ("New

Studies of Post-Pleistocene Human Skeletal Remains from the Rift Valley, Kenya" by GP Rightmire, in, *AJPA 42* (3) 1975 p351-369) corrected this myth. He compared a number of measurements, including biauricular and maximum skull breadth, between Stone Age Kenyans and Bantu-speaking populations and found they were within the range of 'Negroes'. He found no evidence of Eurasian association.

It is such a Kenyan-type population who are the origins of the Tutsi of Rwanda and Burundi. It is such who are the African component amongst Somalis and, to a certain degree, Ethiopians (this is why it is said the Tutsi came from Somalia or Ethiopia and a few Tutsi look like Ethiopians). Somalis and Ethiopians also have a Eurasiatic component. **It would be odd arguing against Eurasian intermixture in the Horn of Africa where the coasts are only 40 miles away from cold-adapted populations. It defies common sense that with those proximities there would be no significant co-mingling.** Our point is that the dominant frequency of narrow noses amongst the Tutsi and Stone Age Kenyans does not suggest Eurasian-African mixing. **In cases where a broad-nosed population meets a narrow-nosed population, in equal amounts, the offspring are dominantly intermediate in nasal breadth.** That is not what we observe amongst Tutsi and Stone Age Kenyans but a dominant narrow-nosed pattern. In any case **no one could sincerely argue** that the Tutsi, with African hair and complexion, look like the result of equal intermixing between Eurasians and Sub-Saharan Africans. Most studies on the effect of climate on nasal shape have not looked at the impact of low humidity in Sub-Saharan Africa.

The first 30 Norwegian male skulls have nasal indices ranging from 43.4 to 57.1 (13.7 range). The first 30 Teita male skulls have indices ranging from 47.3 to 66.7 (19.4 range). **Sub-Saharan Africans usually have the greater variation in their skull measurements.** The average Norwegian male index is **48.7** and that of Teita males is **55.5**. **There is less difference between the averages of these two populations than in the ranges within the populations.** Once again, this is why it is said 'there is no such thing as race'. Human populations are not absolute even in their noses, which are seen as a central characteristic of 'race'.

The pre-dominant pattern in Sub-Saharan Africa is of broad noses in the populations. Most forensic anthropologists expect this pattern when dealing with individuals or populations of Sub-Saharan African origin. Below are the shape of nasal openings they expect to find in European, East Asian and Sub-Saharan African populations and populations of those origins. Broad noses have high indices and are called **platyrrhine**; narrow noses have low indices and are called **leptorrhine**. Intermediate noses are called **mesorrhine.** One anatomist tells us:

> Hinender described three nasal types with typical racial characteristics; platyrrhine (African), mesorrhine (Asian), and Leptorrhine (Caucasian).

Surgical Anatomy of the Face by WF Larrabee, KH Makielski, JL Henderson; Lippincott Williams and Wilkins 2004

Interestingly approximations of these nasal types are seen in the world of primates as can be seen below. **They show the same variety as humans, even in their facial colouring** (yet only **one** human variety gets to be reminded of the similarity).

Figure 15 Humans and primates contain same variety

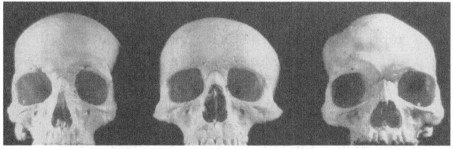
Figure 16 Nasal openings of European, East Asian and African

Judean Nasal Indices

With this in mind let us look at what the Israeli forensic anthropologists had to say about Judeans of the Hellenistic and Roman period.

A relative frequency of **platyrrhiny, 19% to 44% in the males** of the several periods and **40% to 50% in the females** was found. To be sure, the number of crania providing **some** of the indices is **quite small,** and the results must remain tentative.

Arensburg et al (1980) p179

The team of Arensburg defined platyrrhiny as having a nasal index of 51+. On p181 of the above cited paper a table gives the percentage of platyrrhine noses in the Hellenistic period as **44.4%** amongst **21** male skulls and **50%** amongst **16** female skulls. In the Roman period the incidence amongst **29** male skulls was **18.5%** but was **42.8%** amongst **15** female skulls. The ideal minimum for a same-sex sample of skulls is 30 **but the consistency of high percentage amongst females from 16 and then 15 skulls, the sum of which is 31, reaches the ideal minimum. This suggests it is representative of the occurrence of the trait in the population**. Table 5 compares these results with Europeans and Sub-Saharan Africans from the Howells database:

Table 5

Population males (30 skulls)	Nasal Index 51+
Teita, Kenyan	90.0% 27/30
Zulu, South African	93.3% 28/30
Dogon, Malian	100% 30/30
Norse, Norwegian	26.7% 8/30
Zalavar, Hungarian	30.0% 9/30
Berg, Austrian	26.7% 8/30
Gizeh 26-30th dynasty Egyptian	10.0% 3/10

| Lachish (Risdon), Judah | 56.7% 17/30 |
| En Gedi Hellenistic Judean male | 44.4% |

Lachish first 30 male skull measurements are from: "A Study of the Cranial and Other Human Remains From Palestine Excavated at Tell Duweir (Lachish) by the Wellcome-Marston Archaeological Research Expedition" by D. L. Risdon, in, *Biometrika* 31 (1/2) 1939), pp. 99-166

The Lachish Judah nasal indices are neither like Sub-Saharan Africans or Europeans but somewhat closer to the Africans. The nasal indices of Hellenistic period Judeans are also in neither group but are closer to Europeans. **Judging solely by the nasal indices above** the Lachish males are an unequal blend of Afro-type and Euro-type but with more Afro-type. The Hellenistic Judeans of both sexes and Roman females appear to have more Euro-type.

How do we estimate the proportions? Let us assume that the European population involved was like the Hungarians (30% platyrrhiny) and the African population involved was like the Dogon (100% platyrrhiny). Hellenistic period Judean males would be **66.6% European and 33.3% Sub-Saharan African** ([30 + 100]/3 = 43.33%, **1/3 = 33.3% African ancestry**). Hellenistic period Judean females, **assuming the same**, would be **61% European and 38.5% Sub-Saharan African** ([30 + 100]/2.6 = 50%, **1/2.6 or 38.5% African ancestry**). If we assumed the African population involved was like the Teita (90% platyrrhiny) the Judean males would be **63% European and 37% Sub-Saharan African** ([30 + 90]/2.7 = 44.44%, 1/2.7 = 37% African ancestry). Judean females, assuming the same, would be **58.4% European and**

41.7% **Sub-Saharan African** ([30 + 90]/2.4 = 50%, 1/2.4 = 41.7% African ancestry). **The lower the incidence of platyrrhiny, in the African population involved, the higher the proportion of projected African heritage amongst the Judeans.** This is of critical importance because the Afro-type population involved was almost certainly from further north than the Teita or Dogon. As we are about to see African populations from further north have a lower incidence of platyrrhiny because they tend to have lower mean nasal breadths.

Table 6

Population males (30 unless stated)	Mean Nasal Br (mm)
Norse, Norwegian	25.0
Zalavar, Hungarian	25.5
Berg, Austrian	25.7
Poundbury, Roman Britain (50)	25.2
Teita, Kenyan	27.8
Zulu, South African	28.6
Dogon, Malian	28.3
Rwanda (Tutsi) (40)	25.9
C-Group Nubian (2nd Cataract) (22)	25.5
Kerma Nubian (3rd Cataract) (72)	25.8
Gizeh, 26-30th dynasty Egyptians	24.5
Lachish, Judah (700 BC)	25.1

Nubian skull measurements are referenced from "Nubian Identity in the Bronze Age" by Michele R Buzon, in, *Bioarchaeology of the Near East 5* (2011) p28

Lachish skull measurements are from Keita (1988) p382

Rwanda skull measurements are from "Cranial Measurements and Discrete Traits Compared in Distance Studies of African Negro Skulls" by G. P. Rightmire, in, *Human Biology* 44 (2) 1972 pp. 269

A clear division emerges between Sub-Saharan Africans and Europeans which can be put down to differences in environmental temperatures. The Nubians, however, are Saharan latitude Africans and have the same mean nasal breadth as Europeans. We can attribute this to the low humidity of the region they are indigenous to. The low humidity of Northern Sudan is confirmed by the 2009 study of Hubbe et al on p1731 where the relative humidity for Dunqula is **25** (compared to a world average of around 65). Anyone who has seen ancient Egyptian paintings of Nubians will be under no doubt that they were no different to Sub-Saharan Africans in their physical appearance. In other words they were Black. **This puts a different complexion on the very low platyrrhiny percentage and mean nasal breadth of Late Dynastic Egyptians from Gizeh**. Egypt is also arid but with a lower 'coldest temperature' than Sudan (Hubbe et al 2009 p1731). This explains the higher nasal heights of the Lower Egyptians (first 30 males **51.9**) in relation to the Nubians (**49.3**). It seems more natural to compare them to Nubians, their neighbours, than to Europeans.

Table 6 also potentially radically changes the proportion of African in the Judean population. We do not have the figures for the percentage of +51 nasal indices amongst the Nubian skulls. The narrower mean nasal breadth (**25.8**) of Nubians, however, indicates that their platyrrhiny percentage is much lower than amongst the Teita (**27.8**), just as the Teita have a lower percentage, 90%, than the Dogon, 100%, (**28.3**). The Nubians have nasal breadths similar to Europeans but nasal heights comparable to Africans (first 30 Zulu males **49.9**, first 30 Teita males **50.1**, first 30 Dogon **47.5**, C-Group Nubians **49.3**). A reasonable estimate is that the percentage of skulls displaying +51 nasal indices amongst Nubians would be equidistant between the European average and the Sub-Saharan African average percentages. A mean Sub-Saharan percentage of 94.4% and a European one of 27.8% would produce a half-way mark of **61.1%** for Nubians. If a population with a 61.1% occurrence of platyrrhiny encountered a population with 27.8% platyrrhiny at 50-50 levels we could expect an occurrence of **44.5%** in the resulting population. This is almost identical to the observed occurrence of 44.4% in Hellenistic period Judean males. We can conclude, **based on nasal index alone**, that Judean males of the Hellenistic period were **50% African ([61.1 + 27.8]/2 = 44.5, ½ = 50%) and Judean females were 55.6% African ([61.1 + 27.8]/1.8 = 49.4)**. We can also conclude that the **Lachish population was around 62.5% Afro-type and 37.5% Euro-type ([61.1 + 27.8]/1.6 = 55.6, 1/1.6=62.5%)**. We should remember this is **based only on nasal index**.

Nasal Spine

The structure of the nose has aspects that are difficult to measure in millimetres. These are called non-metric or discrete traits. The distribution amongst populations of different climatic zones is commented on:

> ...Caucasoid crania tend to have...a prominent lower border (called the nasal sill) and a **marked nasal spine**...Negroids (black people) there is a lack of a nasal sill; the **nasal spine is absent or very small**...

Handbook of Forensic Medicine by Burkhard Madea; John Wiley and Sons 2014 p186

Of 22 Hellenistic period Judean skulls **18.2% had a 'marked' nasal spine**, a trait which has a high frequency amongst Europeans. **18.2% also had 'none-small' nasal spine**, a trait which has a high frequency amongst Sub-Saharan Africans. A **'medium' nasal spine was found in 63.6% of the sample**. The equal proportion of what might be called typically Caucasian and typically Negroid nasal morphology, alongside a form between the two extremes, **suggests a population of Afro-European descent in roughly equal measure**.

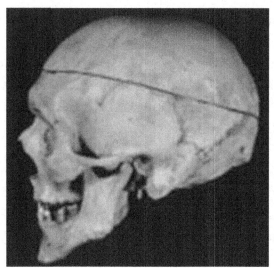

Figure 17 European skull profile, nasal spine is bony protrusion at the bottom of the nose

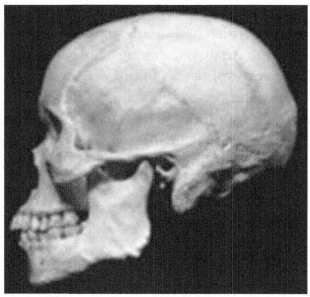

Figure 18 African skull profile showing very small nasal spine

Nasal Bridge and Root

The book *Anthropology* by Ram Nath Sharma and K Sharma has this to say about Sub-Saharan Africans:

> ...it may be stated that **the general Negro nose** is short and very broad with a **slightly depressed root**...

Anthropology by Ram Nath Sharma and Rajendra K Sharma, Atlantic Publishers 2007 p85

The Israeli forensic anthropologists tell us that:

> Nasal Root Depression: **A slight or moderate depression was the most frequently observed**, especially in females.

Arensburg et al (1980b) p286

The same study tells us that 40.7% of Hellenistic period Judean males have 'none-slight' nasal root depression, 40.7% have 'moderate' nasal root depression and 18.5% have this trait in its 'marked' form (Arensburg et al 1980). Even in males this was the dominant pattern. This is also consistent with a mixed population for Hellenistic Judea.

The nasal bridge of 'Negroids' is described as '**broader and flatter**' than those of Caucasoids and Mongoloids (according to *Forensic Art and Illustration* by Karen T Taylor, CRC Press 2010 p62).

Arensburg et al (1980b) p286 describe the Hellenistic period Judean males as having an occurrence of 4.8% long, narrow nasal bridge, 76.2% long, medium width and 19% **short, wide nasal bridge**. This, however, is not the same as indicating a 19% African contribution. The Afro-type involved was more like Nubians, than Sub-Saharan Africans in general, with narrower nasal breadths. Populations with narrower nasal breadths tend to have a higher percentage of narrow-medium nasal bridges and longer nasal bones than populations with broader noses. It is therefore consistent with a mixed population for Hellenistic Judea. Also the percentage of more typically African nasal bridge amongst Hellenistic Judeans is quite similar to that of the more typically African nasal spines, about one in five. This gives the strong impression that the Afro-type involved had both Saharan and Sub-Saharan nasal patterns amongst its people.

Nasal Sill Shape

Regarding the shape of the base of the nasal opening of the skull (nasal sill) there are four possibilities classed as form 1, 2, 3 and 4. The evidence suggests all four forms occur amongst European, East Asian and African populations. We deduce this from the evidence provided by Olaf Krogstad in the paper "The Relationship Between the Lower Margin of the Nasal Aperture and the Maxillary Alveolar Process", in *Zeitschrift fur Morphologie und Anthropologie 65* (1) 1973 p36. We combine it with the data from "Skeletal Remains of Jews from the Hellenistic and Roman Periods in Israel: Non-

Metric Morphological Observations" by MS Goldstein, B Arensburg and H Nathan, in *Bulletin et Memoire de la Societe d'Anthropologie de Paris* 7 (13) 1980b p286. This can be seen in the table below:

Table 7

Population	Form 1	Form 2	Form 3	Form 4
German (191)	23%	5%	69%	3%
Austrian (65)	3%	12%	77%	8%
Tayal, Taiwan (122)	55.1%	12.7%	22%	10.2%
Negro (67)	30%	9%	25%	36%
Hellenistic Judean	20%	20%	60%	0%
Roman Judean	7.1%	14.3%	78.6%	0%

Form 4 does not occur amongst the Judean skulls and occurs with low frequency amongst European and Asian skulls. **The Judeans seem more European in this respect but along with the high frequency of Form 3. In the combined total** of Form 1 and 2 **the Judeans seem more like the 'Negro' than any other population in the table.** This occurrence of the forms amongst Judeans suggests a much stronger Euro-type affinity but could also be interpreted as supporting a mixed population with stronger Euro-type component.

An African population with a higher incidence of narrow noses would have a higher incidence of Form 3 nasal sills and a lower incidence of Form 4. This suggests that the African population involved was more like Nubians.

Conclusion

The nasal indices of Lachish skulls indicated a mixed Afro-Euro-type population with a greater Afro-type component. The Judean skulls indicate an Afro-Euro-type mixture of roughly equal components. The Late Egyptians turn out to be more African than previously suggested because there indices are somewhat reminiscent of Nubians. **The nasal spines** of Judean males suggested an Afro-Euro-type population of roughly equal components. **The nasal bridge** of Judean males suggested an Afro-Euro-type population. **The nasal sills** of the Judeans appear to suggest either a more Euro-type population or a mixed Afro-Euro population in Hellenistic times with a more Euro-type population in Roman times. The combined testimony of all four aspects of the skeletal nose suggests an Afro-Euro-type population in the Judean period of roughly equal blend.

What the Forensic Anthropologists Say about the Nose

> Most importantly, **nasal cavities from cold–dry climates are relatively higher and narrower compared with those of hot–humid climates**, agreeing with previous findings on the nasal aperture. The shape changes found are functionally consistent with an increase in contact between air

and mucosal tissue in cold–dry climates by increase of turbulence during inspiration and increase in surface-to-volume ratio in the upper nasal cavity.
http://134.2.48.77/fileadmin/website/arbeitsbereich/ufg/pal aeoanthropologie/Mitarbeiter/Nobacketal2011.pdf

CHAPTER 5: WHAT THE MID- AND LOWER FACE TELL US

Orbit Shape

April Garwin teaches forensic anthropology and her Lesson 6 deals with *Ancestry Determination*. She has a section called "Summary of the Current Research Methodology" in which she says about 'eye orbit shape':

> Caucasoid; angular and sloping
> Negroid; square or rectangular
> Mongoloid; round and non-sloping
> http://www.redwoods.edu/instruct/agarwin/anth_6_ancestry.htm

The skulls from Hellenistic period Judea were 14.8% round for males and 37.5% round for females; **77.8% (27 skulls) square for males and 56.3% (16 skulls) for females. During the Roman period both sexes 64.3% (14 skulls) have square orbits**. According to this trait the Judean population of En Gedi had stronger Sub-Saharan African affinities than Eurasian to the tune of 66.1% to33.8%.

Prognathism

What is alveolar prognathism and what is the relevance of it to geographical groups? April Garwin informs us that:

Caucasoids have a 'flat' (orthognathous) face in the dental area along the midline. This is the opposite of the Negroid face, which exhibits protrusion of the mouth region, known as prognathism. [...] **Negroids are noted for alveolar prognathism,** or an anterior protrusion, of the mouth region.
http://www.redwoods.edu/instruct/agarwin/anth_6_ancestry.htm

The next question is to what degree does alveolar prognathism arise in the Judean population? Arensburg et al, inform us that:

Moderate to marked upper **alveolar prognathism was not infrequent among En Gedi males,** as well as in the Roman period crania.
Arensburg (1980b) p285

Of the Judean Hellenistic period males 54% had 'none-slight' prognathism but **45.4% had 'moderate-marked' prognathism**. This is in keeping with a mixed population of Afro-Euro-type in roughly equal amounts.

Bizygomatic breadth

The breadth of the face, just beneath the eyes at the mid-ear plane, is called the bizygomatic breadth. This measurement separates the European and African skull samples in the Howells database, as checked by the present author. It also goes a considerable way to separating cold-adapted, warm-

56

located Asians from neighbouring Negritos and Australo-Melanesians, although there is some overlap. Let us compare the bizygomatic breadths of African, European and Judean skulls.

Table 8

Population Males (30)	Bizygomatic Br
Norse, Norwegian	134
Zalavar, Hungarian	133
Berg, Austrian	136.6
Poundbury, Roman Britain (50)	136.4
Teita, Kenyan	131.5
Dogon, West African	129.4
Zulu, South African	129.9
Kerma Nubians (52)	129.7
Lachish, Israel (700 BC) (61)	129.7
Hellenistic Judean	131.6
Roman Judean	132.2
Safed, Galilee 1500 BC (7)	126
Safed, Roman Galilee (14)	129

Poundbury and Lachish data from "Analysis of Crania from Tell Duweir Using Multiple Discriminant Functions" by SOY Keita, *AJPA 75* (1988) p375-390

The Africans, in the above table, have lower bizygomatic breadths than the Europeans. In the samples the lower European limit is **133** while the upper African limit is **131.5**. The difference is approximately 1.5mm. The Lachish Judah males have an average bizygomatic breadth that is identical to that of the Kerma Nubians. The 18th dynasty period male skulls from Safed are firmly within the African range. **The Roman period Safed male skulls, from Galilee, are also within the African range**. The Hellenistic period Judean males are far closer to the African range than they are to the European. The Roman period Judeans, from En Gedi, seem equidistant from Europeans and Africans. It is still possible to argue an Afro-Euro-type population if the Afro-type population had an average of 126, like 18th dynasty Safed, and the Euro-type population had an average of 136.5 like the Berg Austrians. This interpretation would be consistent with most of the other evidence to date.

Conclusion

The orbit shapes among the Judeans show a high frequency of orbit shapes associated with Sub-Saharan Africans. The frequency of moderate-marked **alveolar prognathism** amongst the Hellenistic and Roman Judeans strongly suggests a mixed Afro-Euro-type population of equal blend which became more Euro-type during the Roman period. Risdon did not give percentages of the Lachish population that showed prognathism. **The Bizygomatic breadths** of the Lachish population strongly suggest an Afro-type population. Those of the Judeans suggest a mixed population during the Hellenistic period which became more Euro-type during the Roman period. The combined testimony of all three traits strongly suggests a mixed Afro-Euro-type population.

CHAPTER 6: WHAT BUMPS AND GROOVES ON THE SKULL TELL US

The Origins of Skull Discrete Traits

Most people think of the skull as being one bone. Anyone who has ever held a skull will know that it is made of different parts. They are the frontal bone (at the front of the skull), occipital bone (at the back), two parietal bones which take up most of the sides, two temporal bones, and two sphenoid bones. The universal bones are 8 in all. When you view the skull all of these bones look like they have been sown together. The 'stitch' lines are called **sutures**. They can be simple lines or complex, zigzagging lines.

Sometimes smaller bones develop within sutures but this depends on the **individual**. Skulls can also have grooves, markings and depressions along the surface. The sutural bones and various markings of a skull are collectively called **discrete** or **non-metric traits**. We cannot measure them but simply record whether a given discrete trait is present or not. They can tell us which part of the world a **sample of skulls** is likely to originate from. Two of the world's leading experts in these traits are the forensic anthropologists Berry and Berry. In 1967 they concluded that non-metric traits **measure genetic heritage and population affiliation better than a collection of metric traits** ("Epigenetic Variation in the Human Cranium" by A Caroline Berry and RJ Berry, in, *Journal of Anatomy 101* (2) 1967 p377.

Sutural Complexity of Ancient Jews and Africans

The human skull has a mixture of simple and complex sutural lines. Which ones are simple and which ones are complex appears to have a lot to do with geographical origin. Virginia Sutton, who had a Master's Degree in anthropology in the early 20th century, describes the relationship between geography and sutural complexity:

> In the skull of **the negro the posterior (lambdoidal) suture is most complex**; in **the Caucasian, the frontal (coronal) suture**; while in **the Mongoloid it is the one along the mid-line of the skull (the sagittal)**.
> This is **not** an infallible indication. It is not at all uncommon to find individuals in whom the configuration of the sutures is at variance with the other racial indications of the skull. But for a **long series** the information of the sutures will **usually hold good as a racial criterion**, and in determining race, the relative complexity of the sutures is ordinarily taken into consideration.

"The Sutures of the Mesa Verde Cliff-Dwellers" by Virginia Sutton

http://npshistory.com/nature_notes/meve/vol7-1b.htm

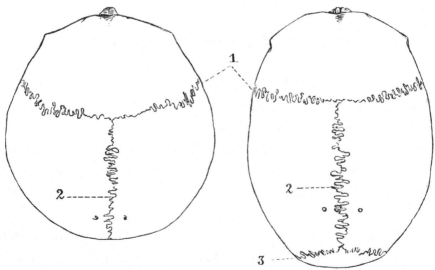

Figure 19 1 is the coronal, 2 is the sagittal and 3 is the lambdoidal suture

For Caucasians we have been told the coronal suture is most complex while the others are relatively simpler. For Sub-Saharan Africans the lambdoidal suture is most complex while the others are relatively simpler. We are also warned about **considerable variation within geographic groups**, something we have seen across every trait for which we have had the necessary data. It is the mean or average for a sample that can be used to suggest ancestry. In the light of this information let us take a look at the non-metric traits of skulls from Judah and Judea.

The skulls of Jews of the Hellenistic and Roman period from En Gedi are described, in terms of their sutures, by forensic anthropologists as having:

Serration in the coronal was predominantly "simple", more so in female than in male crania. The sagittal suture, in contrast, was most frequently moderately complex. **Although the most prevalent kind of serration in the lambdoidal suture was also moderately complex**, a relatively high incidence of **markedly complex saturation was here evident** (17% in the Hellenistic and 21% in the Roman period).

"Skeletal Remains of Jews From The Hellenistic and Roman Periods in Israel: Non-Metric Traits" by MS Goldstein, B Arensburg, and H Nathan, in, Bulletin et Memoir de la Societe d Anthropolgie de Paris 7, serie XIII 1980b p283-84

If we had to make a decision **based solely** on this the dominant 'simple' pattern in the coronal suture would **appear** to make 'Caucasian' identity unlikely. We would have a choice between Sub-Saharan Africans and East Asians. When we consider the distance of Judea from East Asia and Sub-Saharan Africa the latter becomes the clear favourite. The highest incidence of **'markedly complex' was lambdoidal** and not sagittal. This also supports African rather than Asiatic affinity. Thankfully we do not have to make a decision based only on this trait. We have other data.

Metopic Suture

In the skull of a child the two halves of the forehead (frontal bone) are connected by a suture that runs from the top of the nose to the top of the head (end of the frontal bone). It usually closes up completely by the age of 7 but sometimes it persists into adulthood. This is known as **metopism**. A metopic suture in adult skulls is rare enough amongst Sub-Saharan Africans and East Asians for some commentators **to claim it does not occur** (we shall see this is not quite true). It is, however, common amongst Europeans and those of partial Euro-type ancestry in the zones of intermixing. In a study by AC Berry and RJ Berry ("Origins and Relationships of Ancient Egyptians", in, *Journal of Human Evolution Vol 1* 1972) of skull morphology between different populations Ashanti showed 0 cases but prehistoric Nubians showed 3.2% cases. Naqada pre-dynastic Egyptians showed 6.6 %, Lachish Israelites showed 7.4% but Medieval Edinburgh and Oslo showed 18% and 20% respectively. In a study by GP Rightmire on discrete traits (Rightime 1972) the Sotho of South Africa had a metopism occurrence of 4.4%. **Prehistoric Upper Egyptians and Iron Age Israelites were closer to the Sotho and prehistoric Nubians than they were to northern Europeans in the frequency of metopism.** Concerning the Judean skulls from En Gedi we are told:

> **Few crania of adults manifested the metopic suture: 2.3% of the males, none in the females of the En Gedi material, and none in the Roman period crania.** This finding is in sharp contrast to the relatively high frequency of metopism in Bedouin crania from Israel: 18% in males, 24% in females.

Arensburg et al (1980b) p284

It would appear the modern Bedouin of Palestine are closer to European frequencies for this trait than the ancient

Judeans. The ancient Judeans, however, appear to be more like Sub-Saharan Africans than indigenous North Africans, for this trait.

Supraorbital Notch vs Foramen

The supraorbital region of the skull is approximately just beneath the eyebrow on a living person. On this region of the skull two types of mark might occur; a notch or a foramen (opening through which nerve or tissue goes through). Apparently whether it is one or the other has climatic correlation:

> In cold climatic conditions, supraorbital foramina were found in the highest frequency (35.4%). **In warm and temperate climates, the observed frequencies of supraorbital foramen were the lowest (18.8% and 19.9%, respectively). Frequency of supraorbital notches was the lowest of those skulls from a cold climate (44%) and the highest in those from a warm climate (59%).** These results support the hypothesis that the occurrence of supraorbital notches is greater in populations from warm compared with cold regions.

"The Localization of the Supraorbital Notch or Foramen is Crucial for Headache and Supraorbital Neuralgia Avoiding Treatment by A Tomaszewska, Barbera Kwiatkowska and Rimantas Jankauskas, in, *The Anatomical Record 295* (9) 2012 p1494

Skulls from warm and temperate climates have low incidences of supraorbital foramen at around **18-19%**. In the Israelite remains from Lachish we are told:

> The incidence of a supraorbital foramen in the **Lachish crania, 17%** and in the Modern Palestine group, **20.6%** (...)...

Arensburg at al 1980b p287-88

For the Lachish skulls this is an even lower occurrence than what is expected for warm to temperate countries. For the modern Palestinian skulls it was slightly higher. **This associates the Israelite remains with warm-adaptation**. We would expect this from a population with affinities to Sub-Saharan Africans. The Judean skulls from En Gedi had right orbit notches at 76% and 79% in males and females respectively, well in excess of the 59% predicted for warm climates (Arensburg et al 1980 p283).

Berry and Berry

In 1972 Berry and Berry published an extensive study comparing the discrete traits of populations from Africa, Europe and Lachish. Below we have combined the results with those of Rightmire (1972), where the data is available, and shown the results:

Highest Nuchal Line Present
Medieval Scotland 36%
Norway, Oslo 67%

Pre-dynastic Egypt **16.2%**
Prehistoric Nubia **13.3%**
Ashanti 3.6%
Lachish **16.7%**
Conclusion: Frequency of **Lachish skulls is closest to pre-dynastic Upper Egyptians and Nubians**. They are most distant from northern Europeans.

Lambdoidal Ossicle present
Medieval Scotland 47.5%
Norway, Oslo 40%
Prehistoric Nubia 44.6%
Ashanti **25.9%**
Pre-dynastic Egypt **31.6%**
Lachish **29.8%**
Conclusion: Frequency of this trait in **Lachish skulls is closest to pre-dynastic Upper Egyptians and Ashanti**. They are most distant from Prehistoric Nubians and northern Europeans. The Prehistoric Nubians are, interestingly, closer to the northern Europeans for this trait.

Parietal Foramen Present
Norway, Oslo 64%
Medieval Scotland **52%**
Sotho 56.7%
Zulu 68%
Rwanda 65.5%
Ashanti 59.2%
Prehistoric Nubia 56.9%
Pre-dynastic Egypt **53.2%**
Lachish **35%**

Conclusion: Frequency of this trait in Lachish skulls is different from every other group sample. They are **closest to Medieval Scotland and pre-dynastic Upper Egyptians but at a great distance**. They are most distant from Zulu and Tutsi Rwandans.

Metopism
Norway, Oslo 20%
Medieval Scotland 18%
Ashanti 0%
Sotho **4.4%**
Zulu 2%
Rwanda 0%
Prehistoric Nubia 3.2%
Pre-dynastic Egypt **6.6%**
Lachish **7.4%**
Conclusion: Frequency of this trait in **Lachish skulls is closest to pre-dynastic Upper Egyptians and Sotho South Africans**. It is most distant from Europeans.

Epipteric Bone Present
Medieval Scotland 18.5%
Norway, Oslo 18%
Prehistoric Nubia 14.9%
Sotho **8.1%**
Zulu 6.1%
Rwanda **8.2%**
Ashanti 6.2%
Pre-dynastic Egyptians 6.7%
Lachish **9.5%**

Conclusion: Frequency of this trait in **Lachish skulls is closest to Sotho South Africans and Tutsi Rwandans**. They are most different from northern Europeans.

Frontal Temporal Articulation
Prehistoric Nubia 13.2%
Ashanti 9.8%
Medieval Scotland 0%
Pre-dynastic Egyptians **1.1%**
Norway Oslo **1%**
Lachish **0.9%**
Conclusion: Frequency of this trait in the **Lachish skulls is closest to Norwegians and pre-dynastic Upper Egyptians**. It is most different from Prehistoric Nubians and Ashanti.

Parietal Notch Bone Present
Norway, Oslo 12%
Pre-dynastic Egyptians 8.3%
Medieval Scotland 8%
Sotho 12.2%
Zulu 12%
Rwanda 9%
Ashanti **6.2%**
Prehistoric Nubians **0%**
Lachish **2.8%**
Conclusion: Frequency of this trait in **Lachish skulls closest to Prehistoric Nubians and Ashanti**. It is most different from Sotho South Africans, Zulu and Norwegians.

Zygomatico-Facial Foramen
Norway, Oslo 9%

Medieval Scotland 13.4%

Pre-dynastic Egyptians 16.7%

Ashanti **18.7%**

Sotho 80%

Zulu 84%

Rwanda 80.3%

Prehistoric Nubia **40.5%**

Lachish **30%**

Conclusion: Frequency of this trait in **Lachish skulls closest to Prehistoric Nubians and Ashanti**. It is most different from Zulu, Sotho and Tutsi Rwandan.

Supraorbital Foramen

Medieval Scotland 25%

Norway, Oslo 21%

Sotho 28.9%

Zulu 21%

Rwanda 33.6%

Prehistoric Nubians **10.6%**

Ashanti **11.7%**

Pre-dynastic Egypt **11.8%**

Lachish **13.6%**

Conclusion: **Frequency of this trait in Lachish skulls closest to pre-dynastic Upper Egyptians and Ashanti**. It is most different from Rwandan Tutsi and Sotho. **Results contradict the predictions of Tomaszewska et al (2012)**.

Anterior Ethmoid Foramen

Norway, Oslo 29.3%

Medieval Scotland 18.4%

Pre-dynastic Egyptians 17.3%

Ashanti 15.4%

Sotho 1.2%

Zulu **5.1%**

Rwanda 2.5%

Prehistoric Nubians **8%**

Lachish **7.7%**

Conclusion: Frequency of this trait in **Lachish skulls is closest to Prehistoric Nubians and Zulu**. It is most different from northern Europeans.

Table 9

African Closest Two	African Furthest Two
Nuchal line	Frontal-temporal articulation
Lambdoidal ossicle	Zygomatico-Facial foramen
Metopism	Supraorbital foramen
Epipteric Bone	Parietal foramen
Parietal Notch Bone	
Zygomatico-Facial foramen	
Supraorbital foramen	
Anterior Ethmoid Foramen	

Table 10

European Furthest Two	European presence in Furthest Two
Highest Nuchal line	Lambdoidal ossicle
Metopism	Parietal Notch Bone
Epipteric Bone	
Anterior Ethmoid foramen	

Of the nine tabled results of headed discrete traits six compare 6 African samples to 2 European samples while three compare 3 African samples to 2 European ones. **There is also high variability in the frequencies of the traits amongst Africans**. We can, therefore, expect African bias in terms of presence in **both** the 'closest two' and 'furthest two' in relation to the Lachish sample. Instead what we find is a clear African bias in 'closest two' **in contrast** to 'furthest two'. We also find a clear European bias in 'furthest two' **in contrast** to 'closest two'. **There are no European 'closest two' examples**. The greater number of African samples has not prevented clear patterns of distance, in relation to the Lachish sample, from emerging. **Lachish can only be classed as being closer to the Africans than the Europeans**.

Conclusion

The sutural complexity of Judean skulls suggests an affinity with Sub-Saharan Africans. The frequency of supraorbital notches suggests a very warm-adapted affinity. The supraorbital foramen frequency suggests Sub-Saharan African affinity. Judean skulls, on this evidence, are warm-adapted and have Sub-Saharan and Saharan African affinity.

The Lachish skulls also show Sub-Saharan and Saharan African affinities more than European ones. For the frequency of 'highest nuchal line present' Lachish skulls are **closest to pre-dynastic Upper Egyptians and Nubians**. For

71

the frequency of 'lambdoidal ossicle present' Lachish skulls are **closest to pre-dynastic Upper Egyptians and Ashanti**. For the 'parietal foramen' trait Lachish skulls are **closest to Medieval Scottish and pre-dynastic Upper Egyptian**. For the frequency of 'metopism' Lachish skulls are **closest to pre-dynastic Upper Egyptians and Sotho South Africans**. For the frequency of 'epipteric bone present', Lachish skulls are **closest to Sotho South Africans and Tutsi Rwandans**. For the frequency of 'frontal-temporal articulation' Lachish skulls are **closest to Norwegians and pre-dynastic Upper Egyptians**. For the frequency of 'parietal notch bone present' the Lachish skulls are **closest to Prehistoric Nubians and Ashanti**. For the frequency of 'zygomatico-facial foramen' Lachish skulls are **closest to Prehistoric Nubians and Ashanti**. For the frequency of 'supraorbital foramen' Lachish skulls are **closest to pre-dynastic Upper Egyptians and Ashanti**. For the frequency of 'anterior ethmoid foramen' Lachish skulls are **closest to Prehistoric Nubians and Zulu. There is considerable overlap for individual traits but the combined evidence makes a clear statement.**

Europeans are never the 'closest two' but are the 'furthest two' four times. Little else need be said to stress the African association of Lachish discrete skull traits.

CHAPTER 7: THE CONCLUSIONS OF OTHERS ON ANCIENT ISRAEL

Lachish

There have been a number of studies done on the Lachish skulls. The studies conducted by Keita in 1988 and by Ulinger and colleagues in 2005 stand out. The former was based on **skull measurements** while the latter concentrated on **discrete features of the teeth**. Just as the skull has bumps and grooves which reveal something of the owner's genetic heritage so do the teeth. Since the present author has made his own conclusions on the Lachish skulls it pays to investigate the conclusions of these studies.

Skulls

Ulinger and colleagues studied the teeth of skulls from two Israeli archaeological sites; Lachish and Dothan. They started by giving a robust summary of previous studies on Lachish skull measurements. In the introduction they inform us that:

> Utilizing craniometrics, Risdon (1939) concluded that the group was very similar to dynastic Egyptian material. In fact, he stated that **the entire population was of foreign origin, representing descendants of a group derived primarily from Upper Egypt**. This conclusion was **subsequently supported** by a

craniometric study by Musgrave and Evans (1981). Keita (1988, p. 377) likewise examined the skulls metrically, omitting those that were either "artificially deformed, female, warped, split, [or] juvenile," using only those measurements that he believed were consistent population discriminators. He concluded that **the group was fairly heterogeneous, having close relationships to North African, Egyptian, and Nubian groups**, thus lending support to an "Egypto-Nubian presence"(Keita, 1988, p. 388). p468

AJPA 128 (2005)

"Bioarchaeological Analysis of Cultural Transition in the Southern Levant Using Dental Nonmetric Traits" by JM Ulinger et al

http://www3.nd.edu/~sheridan/Dothan.pdf

What Risdon actually said was that Lachish skulls were closest to **18ᵗʰ dynasty Upper Egyptians as opposed to pre-dynastic Upper Egyptians.** The difference was that the 18ᵗʰ dynasty skulls were less prognathic and more wider-skulled as if influenced by the Lower Egyptians. Keita concluded that Egyptians and Nubians were probably present in Lachish based on the skull measurements. He also cited the Bible as evidence that Egypto-Nubians were fighting the Assyrians, eventual destroyers of Lachish, in Judah. Keita saw great variety in the skulls of Lachish. He ran an individual skull analysis to see which geographical group the Lachish skulls would class into. Lachish was one of the options in this analysis. Keita reported:

The reclassification results show the Lachish series to have the greatest number of misclassifications, with only 39.3% being correctly classified...Approximately 31% misclassified into **coastal North African** and **northern Egyptian series**, and **30% into southern Egyptian, Nubian, and tropical African series**.
Keita (1988) p384

A second classifying analysis, without the option of Lachish, was run by Keita:

In the unknown analysis approximately half classified into **northern Egyptian, coastal North African** and European series and the other half into **southern Egyptian, Nubian, and other tropical African series**.
Keita (1988) p384

These results are certainly in keeping with our conclusions on the Lachish skulls that they were of Afro-Euro-type with a **dominant** Afro-type component. If anything they suggest a **predominant** Afro-type component. Let us look at the groups Lachish skulls classed into with the benefit of another Keita paper to help interpret ("Studies of Ancient Crania from Northern Africa" by SOY Keita, in *AJPA 83* 1990 p35-48). 'Tropical African' is essentially Sub-Saharan African. 'Nubian' is essentially a Saharan-type African. 'Southern Egyptian', particularly if pre-dynastic, is another Saharan-type African. 'Northern Egyptian' appears to be a mixture of Saharan-type African with a Euro-type (Keita 1990). 'Coastal North African' also appears to be another mixture of Saharan-type with Euro-type (Keita 1990). From a geographical point of view this makes perfect sense. Keita's study strongly suggests that **half of Lachish classed into mixed Afro-Euro-type while the other half classed into Saharan-type African**. We should remember that Saharan-type Africans are not a different 'race' from Sub-Saharan Africans. The traits that they have also occur in Sub-Saharans but in lower frequencies. The former originate from the latter and both have heavily pigmented skins.

Teeth

The conclusion of the Ulinger and colleagues teeth study has been interpreted by some as contradicting the Keita study:

> The results of this dental morphology study **indicate biological continuity in the Late Bronze-Early Iron Age transition in the southern Levant**. The similarity between Tell Dothan and Lachish suggests that the two are more closely related to each other than to other sites in the Mediterranean region...
> The data also indicate that **the group at Lachish maybe more homogenous than previously thought**, while the individuals in the family tomb at Dothan may have been influenced by peoples from the Mediterranean.

p474
http://www3.nd.edu/~sheridan/Dothan.pdf

Does it really? It speaks of greater 'Mediterranean' influence at Dothan, which is further north and, therefore, not surprising. It speaks of continuity in the current region of Israel. Any region which has not suffered a violent invasion and extermination of the population will likely show continuity. This is the case with Egypt also. Why? It is because the population changes have been gradual and dual in nature. On the one hand the first settled people in Upper Egypt, the Badarians (4500 BC), are reported by Keita to have been **tropically-adapted**. The implication is that they were arrivals from further the tropical, rather than sub-tropical, zone. They had nasal heights of around **47.1**. Egypt is in the sub-tropical zone and has **colder winter temperatures** than the tropics. Over a thousand or two thousand year period changes took place amongst the Upper Egyptians. The nasal heights of Naqadans (3500 BC) and Abydos Egyptians (3100 BC) are **51.3** and **53.2** respectively (see Keita 1988 p383). The increase in nasal height can be explained by an adaptation to the colder winter temperatures in a dry climate if we take the correlations of Hubbe et al (2009) into account. The maximum cranial breadth also increased from **132.2** during the Badarian to **134.7** (Naqadan) and then **136.2** during the 1st dynasty. This can be seen as part of the same adaptation. Both nasal height and max skull breadth were changing. During the 26th to 30th dynasty maximum skull breadth was **139.5** but the nasal height **52.8** had decreased from the 1st dynasty. An explanation would be if the difference, after the 1st dynasty, was not because of local evolution but the steady trickle of Asiatic settlers from more northern regions from the Late Old Kingdom onwards. There is abundant evidence from contemporary Egyptian literature for these population movements. The Europeans in the Howell's database had lower nasal heights than Abydos Egyptians and wider maximum skull breadths. A contribution to Lower Egypt from a Euro-type population would account better for the change we see in Egypt when comparing 1st dynasty to Late Lower Dynastic skulls.

It is highly likely that a similar process was taking place in Syro-Palestine and that the south was the last part to experience the change from predominant Afro-type to dominant Euro-type mixture. There was continuity of both population and archaeology in Egypt and Israel with the occasional invasion but it was never followed by extermination. In conclusion the Ulinger et al paper in no way invalidates the evidence of sub-tropical adaptation of the Lachish population and this being the dominant component.

Hellenistic and Roman Judea

Reconstruction Testimony

No study is complete without dealing with the potentially opposing arguments. In recent years reconstructions of Biblical Period Judeans have been conducted. The results have received plenty of media attention.

The present report deals with reconstructing the facial shapes of ancient inhabitants of Israel based on their cranial remains. The skulls of a male from the Hellenistic period and a female from the Roman period have been reconstructed. They were restored using the most recently developed programs in anthropological facial reconstruction, especially that of the Institute of Ethnology and Anthropology of the Russian Academy of Sciences.

"Facial Image of Biblical Jews from Israel" by E Kobyliansky, T Balueva, E Veselovskaya, B Arensburg; in *Anthroplogischer Anzeiger 66* (2) 2008p167

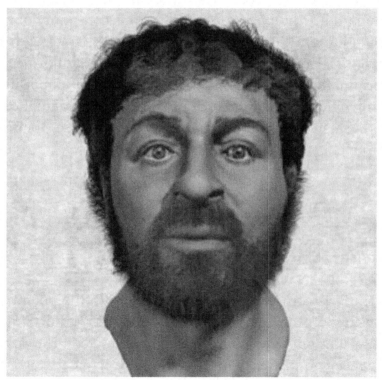

Figure 20 BBC reconstruction of a male skull from 1st century AD. Features should be slightly more generous than they already are, hair should be very curly and skin a little darker

Figure 21 Reconstruction of Roman period Judean from En Gedi. Features should be thicker than they already are, hair should be Semi-Moorish and she should be given a (rich) complexion

Figure 22 Reconstruction of En Gedi Hellenistic period man. Same issues

We should always bear some things in mind when looking at a reconstruction.

1) The **complexion** and **hair** are given at the discretion of the reconstructor.

2) The degree of **broadness of the nose** and **thickness of the lips** are influenced by the reconstructor's perception of the geographical grouping to which the skeleton belonged. Reconstruction guidelines for the noses of skulls designated 'Negroid' are a few millimetres more than for those designated 'Caucasoid'. As a result of this if a skull has a nasal breadth of 27 then it will receive a narrower reconstructed nose if they think it belonged to a White person than if they think the owner was Black or of Black heritage. In short, **the preconceptions of the reconstructor will dominate the appearance of the reconstruction**. Did they use 'Caucasoid' or 'Negroid' reconstructing guidelines?

> ...**width of nose and mouth**...were calculated according to the equations of regression...These equations were formulated by us earlier when researching **populations of European origin**.

Kobyliansky et al (2008) p173

The real question, however, is whether the skeletal evidence of the reconstructed individual supports that conclusion. Both skulls were mesocephalic. We are told of the first, a Hellenistic period male:

The nasal curvature is straight and the **nasal spine is well developed**...the **nasal breadth is of medium size**...Notably the **nose is prominent, long,** and the **nasal bridge is high**...**The alveolar prognathism points to more protruding lips**... The set of attributes of an alveolar part enabled us to reconstruct **a wide mouth with a low and prominent upper lip, with slightly swelling lip blooms**.

Kobyliansky et al (2008) p178-81

This is a combination of Euro-type and Afro-type skeletal features of the face. If anything they should have used both European and African regressive equations to calculate the nose and lip size and then implemented an intermediate reconstruction to reflect the obvious mixed heritage. **They actual admit the Afro-Euro-type heritage of the Roman period woman.** They describe her in the following:

> Her face is oval, low, with a sharp horizontal and vertical profile, of medium width. The **nasal and gnathic parts of the face are prominent,** and **prognathism is strongly developed. The nose is prominent, short, and of medium breadth**...Having a set of the features of an alveolar part of the face enabled us to **reconstruct a big mouth with a high and prominent upper lip, and 'plump' lip blooms**... Based on the description of the skull and the reconstructed facial peculiarities of the woman, we may conclude that she certainly belongs to a **Caucasoid type,** however, **with some original features of an equatorial group**...At the same time,

this person had a very original beauty characterized by a **combination of European features with a southern equatorial ones considered 'plump'**...
Kobyliansky et al (2008) p185-86

The only difference between the man and woman is that the man has a dominant Euro-type component in his mixture whereas the woman has an equal amount of the two components. It does not seem justified to conclude that she belongs to the 'Caucasoid' group. Judging by the percentages of prognathism and platyrrhiny we saw in chapter 4 and 5 she was far from the only one with an equal blend in the Roman period.

Figure 23 Miss Israel 2014, probable appearance of Lachish Judah people

Figure 24 Probable appearance of the average
Hellenistic and Roman period Judean

Conclusion

The conclusion of Keita is that half of the skull sample from Lachish, Judah has southern affinities like southern Egyptians and Nubians. The other half has affinities with coastal North Africans and northern Egyptians. The northerners are themselves a mix of European-like skulls and tropical African-like skulls and those with both characteristics. This strongly suggests that the Lachish skulls were half Afro-type and half Semi-Afro-type. **Alternatively we could conclude that three quarters of the population were Afro-type and a quarter was Euro-type**. Ulinger and colleagues' conclusion that Lachish was probably homogeneous in their ancestry might support the former. **We do not see the Lachish population as expatriate**

but as representing the native Hebrew population. The En Gedi skulls seem like the Lachish skulls but with a higher Euro-type component, in equal blend in the Hellenistic period becoming more Euro-type in the Roman period. Keita's conclusions are broadly consistent with our own findings.

The reconstructions of a Hellenistic period skull and a Roman period skull from En Gedi show a blend of Euro-type and Afro-type traits. In the former there were more Euro-type traits but in the latter there was an even blend. Unfortunately this reality did not inform the reconstruction itself, resulting in the reconstructions looking more Euro-type than they should. The skeletal traits recorded by the forensic anthropologists are broadly consistent with our own conclusions.

CONCLUSION

Most forensic anthropologists use anywhere between 14 and 40 measurements to determine ancestry in a skull. We have found that only a few consistently separate African from European populations and that these are most suitable to apply to ancient Israeli skulls. Geographically Israel is located on the doorstep of Africa so African affinity should really come as no surprise, even though for many it almost certainly does.

The **maximum skull breadth, horizontal circumference, biauricular breadth, bizygomatic breadth** and **nasal indices** all strongly suggest an Afro-Euro-type population with a dominant Afro-type component. The Miss Israel of 2014 is probably the best approximation of what the Lachish Judah people looked like. The Judeans of the Hellenistic period were an equal blend of Afro- and Euro-type and probably approximated the appearance of Barack Obama. Discrete nasal traits of **nasal spine, bridge, root** and **sill** all supported a mixed population with some favouring a stronger Afro-type component and others a Euro-type component. Other discrete traits such as alveolar prognathism and orbit shape support this conclusion.

Ten discrete skull traits were also reviewed and the evidence strongly suggests that the ancient Lachish population had a stronger Sub-Saharan and Saharan African than European affinity. It also suggests that the Judean Hellenistic and Roman period populations had a clear African affinity.

The conclusions of previous studies all show Lachish skulls to have tropical, sub-tropical and mixed affinities. They broadly agree with our own conclusions. The forensic evidence is proof of the assertion made in volume I that the Biblical Old Testament Hebrews were Black and progressively became mixed from the transition of the Old Testament period to the Roman period.

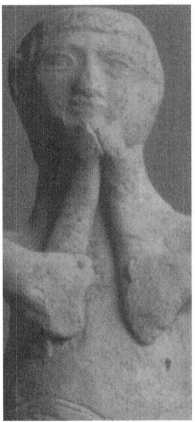

Figure 23 A sculpture from Judah, contemporary with Lachish. Compare with features of Miss Israel

Figure 24 The Annunciation from the catacombs of Priscilla, depicting Mary and Gabriel with rich complexions. More Afro-type than Euro

Figure 25 Scene of Moses and the Israelites crossing the Red Sea from the 2nd century AD Synagogue of Dura/Europos near the Euphrates. Notice hair texture of Moses. Afro-Euro-types

Figure 26 Mosaic from the floor of Beth Alpha Synagogue, 6th century. Very curly hair and rich complexions unmistakable

Figure 27 Beth Alpha Synagogue showing Afro-Euro mixed type

Like our Facebook Page:
https://www.facebook.com/PomegranatePublishing

**OTHER TITLES FROM THE POMEGRANATE LIBRARY
INCLUDE:**

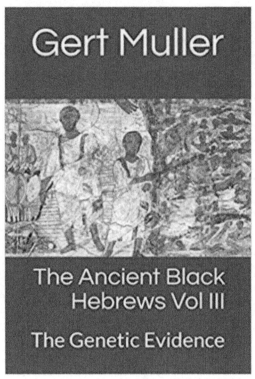

https://www.amazon.com/Ancient-Black-Hebrews-Vol-III/dp/1723831093/

Newly Published!!!

In this volume Muller explains in plain language how genetic evidence proves the ancient Israelites were Black. There is also a section devoted to the Lemba Jews of Africa whose authenticity has recently come under attack. Muller defends the Lemba evidence admirably. Every Black person should read this book!

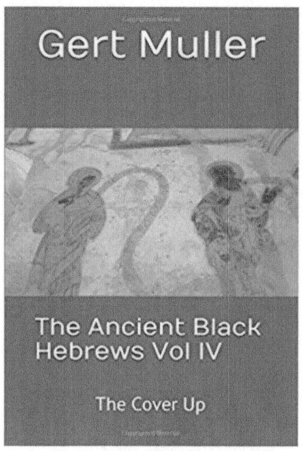

Newly published!!!

The oldest synagogue in the world has proof the first Biblical Jews were Black! This knowledge continued right up to the Middle Ages and we present evidence of a cover up!!!

BLACK ORIGIN ANCIENT GREE CIVILIZATION

GERT MULLER

http://www.amazon.com/Black-Origins-Ancient-Greek-Civilization/dp/1492293261/

WE FOUNDED THEIR FIRST CIVILIZATION! GREAT BUY!

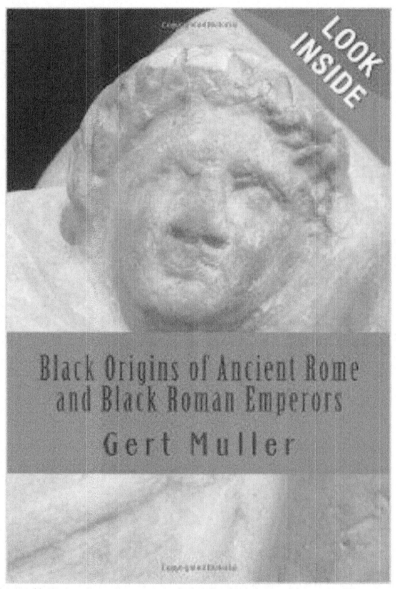

WE FOUNDED THEIR SECOND CIVILIZATION TOO! GREAT BUY!

EVERYTHING YOU WANT TO KNOW ABOUT THE GREATEST
BLACK ECONOMIC ACHIEVEMENT IN THE DIASPORA!!!

THE BEST STARTING PLACE FOR LEARNING ABOUT BLACK HISTORY

INDIA'S FIRST GODS AND CIVILIZATION WERE BLACK!

Black Sumer: The Physical Evidence (Part One)

Hermel Hermstein

http://www.amazon.com/Black-Sumer-Physical-Evidence-ebook/dp/B00BK9X7SC/

http://www.amazon.com/Black-Sumer-Physical-Evidence-Part/dp/1482639440/

ANCIENT EGYPT WAS BLACK. NOW ANCIENT SUMER IS SHOWN TO HAVE BEEN TOO USING CSI LEVEL OF PROOF! THE RACIST IS FAST RUNNING OUT OF CIVILIZATIONS! GREAT BUY!

Black Sumer: The Physical Evidence (Part Two)

Hermel Hermstein

THE ANCIENT ANUNNAKI HAD THE SAME COMPLEXION AS ANCIENT NUBIANS! THEY KEPT THAT ONE QUITE! GREAT BUY!

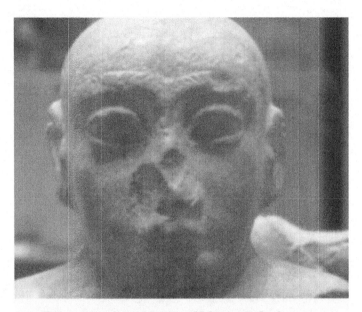

Black Sumer: The African
Origins of Civilisation
Hermel Hermstein

FOR THOSE WHO WANT TO AVOID AN AFRICAN ORIGIN OF CIVILIZATION SUMER, IN SOUTHERN IRAQ, HAS BEEN A SAFE ALTERNATIVE. NOT ANYMORE! THE LAST HIDING PLACE HAS BEEN TAKEN! GREAT BUY!

THE ANCIENT BLACK HEBREWS AND ARABS

THE ANCIENT ARABS AND HEBREWS DIDN'T LOOK LIKE
SADDAM HUSSEIN AND CHARLTON HESTON! GREAT BUY!

WHY WAS IT SOOOO IMPORTANT TO CHANGE THE COLOUR FROM BLACK TO WHITE? GREAT BUY!

THE WORLD'S FIRST CIVILIZATIONS WERE UNMISTAKABLY BLACK! SEE THE PROOF IN 140 COLOUR PICTURES IN ONE PAPERBACK! DEFINITELY ONE FOR THE LIBRARY! GREAT BUY!

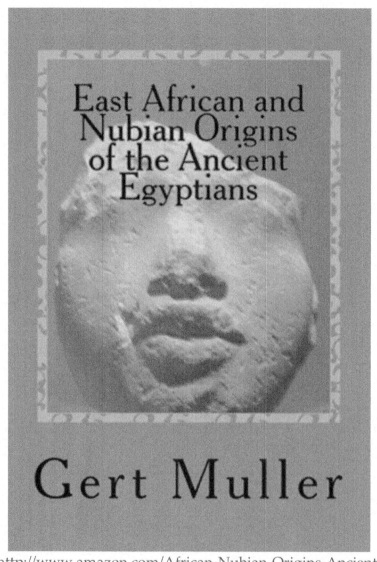

East African and
Nubian Origins
of the Ancient
Egyptians

Gert Muller

OSIRIS, HORUS, AMUN, HATHOR AND THE MAJOR EGYPTIAN
DEITIES WERE ALL FROM THE FAR SOUTH.
THE ANCIENT EGYPTIANS KNEW THAT THE WORLD WAS
ROUND! GREAT BUY!

EDEN: THE BIBLICAL GARDEN DISCOVERED IN EAST AFRICA

GERT MULLER

FOR THOSE WHO WANT TO AVOID AN AFRICAN ORIGIN OF HUMANITY THE BIBLE IS ASSUMED TO BE A SAFE REFUGE. FALSE ASSUMPTION!

EAST AFRICA IS THE GARDEN OF EDEN AND THE LAND OF PUNT. EVERY TEMPLE OF THE ANCIENT EGYPTIAN, GREEK AND ROMAN WORLD WAS INTENDED TO BE A MICROCOSM OF ETHIOPIA.

LEARN ABOUT THE SACRED LONGITUDE AND THE SOURCE OF BIBLICAL MIRACLES! GREAT BUY!

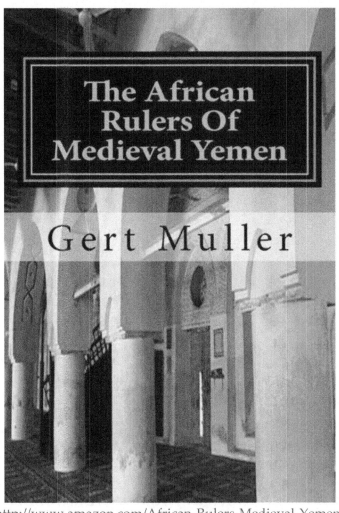

WHAT IS MORE IMPRESSIVE: TO BECOME A KING HAVING COME FROM A LONG LINE OF KINGS OR TO BECOME A KING HAVING COME FROM A LONG LINE OF THE ENSLAVED? GREAT BUY!

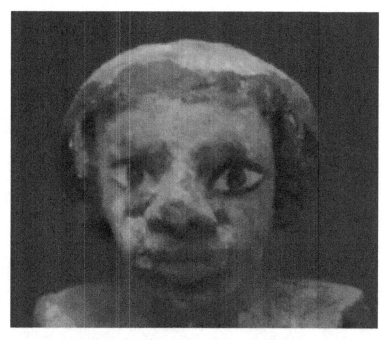

RACIAL UNITY OF THE ANCIENT EGYPTIANS AND NUBIANS

Gert Muller

WHAT COLOUR WERE THE ANCIENT EGYPTIANS? GUESS THIS FACE SETTLES THE QUESTION! GREAT BUY!!!

AFRO HAIR OF THE ANCIENT EGYPTIANS AND BLACKHEADS, AFRICANS OF MESOPOTAMIA

ANU M'BANTU

http://www.amazon.com/Ancient-Egyptians-Blackheads-Africans-Mesopotamia/dp/1499139136/

THE CONTENTIOUS MATTER OF EGYPTIAN HAIR HAS FINALLY BEEN SETTLED!

ANCIENT EGYPTIAN HAIRSTYLES IN EUROPE 30 000
YEARS AGO! WHY? BECAUSE ALL HUMANS ARE OF
AFRICAN ORIGIN!!!

EVERYONE HAS HEARD OF ATLANTIS BUT FEW NO IT
WAS A BLACK CIVILIZATION!!!

Black Civilizations of
the Ancient World: The
Afro-Canaanites
Anu M'Bantu

THE BRILLIANT CIVILIZATION OF THE PHOENICIANS
WAS FOUNDED BY AFRO-CANAANITES!!!

Black Civilizations of the Ancient World: Empire of Carthage

Anu M'Bantu

https://www.amazon.com/Black-Civilizations-Ancient-World-Carthage/dp/1523861509/

THE BRILLIANT CIVILIZATION OF CARTHAGE WHCH FOUGHT ROME WAS A BLACK CIVILIZATION!!!

https://www.amazon.com/Black-Civilizations-Southeast-Asia-Austro-Asiatic/dp/1502835045/

THE CIVILIZATIONS OF SOUTHEAST ASIA WERE BUILT BY PEOPLE OF AUSTRALO-MELANESIAN APPEARANCE!!!

Art of the
Ancient Black
Hebrews

DJEHUTI
HERAKHUTI

EVIDENCE NOONE CAN DENY!

DJEHUTI HERAKHUTI

BLACK AND
BEAUTIFUL
THE MAGNIFICENT ART OF
ANCIENT CIVILIZATIONS

From the ancient civilizations of Egypt, Cyprus, Mesopotamia, Anatolia, India and China beautiful Black sculptures and paintings are presented.